PETS

GUINEA PIGS

by Mari Schuh

AMICUS | AMICUS INK

teeth

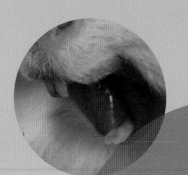

food dish

Look for these
words and pictures
as you read.

claws

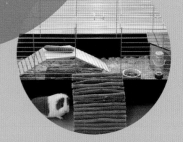

cage

Squeak! Squeak!
A guinea pig is loud.
It wants a treat.

Do you see the teeth?
Guinea pigs are rodents.
They have long front teeth.

teeth

These pets gnaw on wood.
It keeps their teeth healthy.

Do you see the food dish?
Guinea pigs eat pellets.
They also eat hay every day.

food dish

Do you see the claws?
They are short.
Owners trim them.

claws

Do you see the cage?
It is big. Guinea pigs
need room to play.

cage

Now the guinea pig hides.
Peek! It will come out soon!

Do you see the teeth?
Guinea pigs are rodents.
They have long front teeth.

teeth

Do you see the food dish?
Guinea pigs eat pellets.
They also eat hay every day.

food dish

teeth

food dish

Did you find?

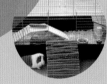

claws

cage

Do you see the claws?
They are short.
Owners trim them.

claws

Do you see the cage?
It is big. Guinea pigs
need room to play.

cage

Spot is published by Amicus and Amicus Ink
P.O. Box 1329, Mankato, MN 56002
www.amicuspublishing.us

Library of Congress Cataloging-in-Publication Data
Names: Schuh, Mari C., 1975- author.
Title: Guinea pigs / by Mari Schuh.
Description: Mankato, Minnesota : Amicus, [2019] | Series:
   Spot. Pets | Audience: K to grade 3.
Identifiers: LCCN 2017029532 (print) | LCCN 2017029934
   (ebook) | ISBN 9781681514505 (pdf) | ISBN
   9781681513683 (library bound) | ISBN 9781681522883
   (paperback)
Subjects: LCSH: Guinea pigs as pets--Juvenile literature. |
   Guinea pigs--Behavior--Juvenile literature.
Classification: LCC SF459.G9 (ebook) | LCC SF459.G9 S38
   2019 (print) | DDC 636.935/92--dc23
LC record available at https://lccn.loc.gov/2017029532

Printed in China

HC   10 9 8 7 6 5 4 3 2 1
PB   10 9 8 7 6 5 4 3 2 1

*To Cami and Avery, who take such great
care of Pedro the Guinea Pig —MS*

Wendy Dieker, editor
Deb Miner, series designer
Ciara Beitlich, book designer
Holly Young, photo researcher

All photos courtesy of Alamy except
AgeFotostock 8-9; iStock cover, 1;
Shutterstock 3, 6-7

GUINEA PIG